This book is presented to:

_____

Family Activity on page 15 is adapted from Liana Lowenstein, ed., *Creative
Family Therapy Techniques: Play, Art, and Expressive Activities to Engage
Children in Family Sessions* (Toronto, ON: Champion Press, 2010), 93.

10 Days of the Easter Story

A Family Experience Through the Feelings of Holy Week

Dr. Josh and Christi Straub

Illustrated by Angelika Scudamore

B&H kids

Brentwood TN

Introduction

The resurrection of Jesus Christ is the most remarkable miracle in history. He conquered death so we, too, will be made alive (1 Corinthians 15:20–22). But the events leading up to Jesus' death were incredibly emotional for His family, disciples, and all who followed Him.

One way we can connect modern-day children to the two-thousand-year-old stories of Jesus is to help them understand the emotions surrounding Holy Week. We can ask them to imagine what they might feel if put in that moment in history.

This is the heart behind *10 Days of the Easter Story*: to introduce your children to the people, events, and feelings from the Triumphal Entry all the way to the ascension. To bring the Easter story alive so children will know they're not alone in their feelings. To realize that we have a Lord who understands our joys and sorrows (Hebrews 4:15).

Why Feelings?

We all have God-given emotions. But our feelings will eventually control our behavior if we deny or suppress them. That's why we must acknowledge what we are feeling, name our emotions, and respond—not react—to them. Teaching our kids to filter their feelings through the lens of the biblical narrative—the active and alive Word of God—has the power to shape their hearts.

Our hope is that your child relates to the characters in the Easter story and *feels* the significance of the moment. These events of Holy Week are not only historical, but they are also transformational and have the power to change hearts.

How to Read 10 Days of the Easter Story

We suggest you begin reading on Palm Sunday. The *"10 Days"* refers more to the time your family will spend with the story than to the chronological events of the biblical account. Not everyone agrees on the exact chronological order of events of Holy Week, but we held to the general timeline.

This book is designed for families with children ages four to ten, but please tailor the stories, activities, and experiences to fit your kids and your schedule. We include pages to record memories and to answer the Family Time Questions so this book can become a keepsake to experience together each Easter.

May these stories prepare your family's hearts to experience Jesus' resurrection, and may the memories bring you joy for years to come. Happy Easter!

Josh and Christi

Timeline of the Holy Week

Day 1
The Triumphal Entry
Happiness
Page 4

Day 2
The Temple
Anger
Page 10

Day 3
The Anointing at Bethany
Gratitude
Page 16

Day 4
The Last Supper
Surprise
Page 22

Day 7
The Unknown
Fear
Page 40

Day 6
The Crucifixion
Sadness
Page 34

Day 5
The Betrayal
Disgust
Page 28

Day 8
The Resurrection
Joy
Page 46

Day 9
Peter's Restoration
Remorse
Page 52

Day 10
The Disciples' Call
Bravery
Page 58

The whole crowd of the disciples began to praise God joyfully with a loud voice for all the miracles they had seen: "Blessed is the King who comes in the name of the Lord."

—Luke 19:37–38

The Triumphal Entry

Read Matthew 21:1–11.

The Triumphal Entry is when Jesus rode into Jerusalem on a donkey as people happily waved palm branches and shouted, "Hosanna! Blessed is He who comes in the name of the Lord—the King of Israel."

Welcome to Day 1 of the Easter story! On this day, Jesus took a journey called the Triumphal Entry. He rode a foal (a young donkey that had never been ridden before) into Jerusalem (Zechariah 9:9). For those who recognized Jesus as the Messiah, this was a day of happiness!

The Triumphal Entry was on the first day of Passover, a Jewish celebration of when God had rescued the Israelites from Egyptian slavery hundreds and hundreds of years earlier. The Jewish people were now under the control of the powerful and cruel Roman Empire. The people thought Jesus, who they saw as the coming King, would finally rescue them again, this time from the Romans.

As Jesus rode into Jerusalem, "the whole crowd of disciples began to praise God joyfully." They shouted "Hosanna!" which means "Save us!" And they said, "Blessed is he who comes in the name of the Lord—the King of Israel" (Luke 19:37; John 12:13).

As a sign of victory, the crowd placed palm branches on the ground in front of Jesus. Not everybody believed He was the Messiah. But His disciples saw Jesus as their victorious King and were happy He had come to save them. They didn't understand that Jesus hadn't come to defeat the Romans; He had come to triumph over sin and Satan and death so we all might be saved and live with God. That was the real triumph brought by this King.

Happiness and the Triumphal Entry

The week leading up to the death and resurrection of Jesus was named *Holy Week* by the church. Palm Sunday is the first day of Holy Week. It is a happy day for those who believe in Jesus—a day we celebrate Jesus' triumph over sin and death.

But not everyone was happy on the first Palm Sunday. The Pharisees, kind of like Christmas grinches, tried to shut down the happiness, asking Jesus to scold His disciples for their loud praise. But Jesus answered, "I tell you, if they were to keep silent, the stones would cry out" (Luke 19:40). How cool is that? All of creation is made to worship God! On Palm Sunday, people were happy to worship and welcome their long-awaited King.

Happiness

Happiness is a feeling, so it comes and goes based on what's happening in our lives. If circumstances change, we may no longer be happy. Unfortunately, just a few short days after the Triumphal Entry, even some of the people who were happy about Jesus would turn on Him and want Him to die.

Prayer

Lord Jesus, I am happy that You came to earth as a King and Savior. Thank You so much! Help me always remember that You came to save me so I can be part of Your Kingdom.

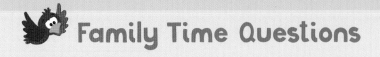 Family Time Questions

1. Imagine you were there the day Jesus rode the donkey into Jerusalem. Where do you picture yourself in the story?

_____

_____

_____

_____

2. What would you be feeling as you saw Jesus riding in front of you on the path?

_____

_____

_____

_____

3. Why do you think the Pharisees weren't happy?

_____

_____

_____

_____

4. Was there ever a time in your life you were happy one day and not so happy the next? What changed?

_____

_____

_____

_____

5. Is there anything you'd like to say to Jesus right now? Put your words into a prayer to Him.

_____

_____

_____

_____

_____

_____

Family Activity

The Happiness Ball

Get a colorful beach ball. On each of the colors of the ball, use a marker to write a phrase. For instance, you could write prompts like:

- Tell about a time when you felt happy.
- Show everyone how you express happiness on the outside.
- Sing a song that makes you happy.
- What do Mom and Dad look like when they are happy?
- Name one thing you feel in your body when you are happy.
- Tell about a time when you got angry with someone but the anger quickly went away because you laughed together.
- Tell about a time someone spoke about you that made you feel happy. What did they say?
- What makes you happy when you are feeling down?

Feel free to make up your own prompts to get your kids talking. As they throw the ball to each other, they answer the prompt closest to their right pointer finger.

Day 2
Feeling:
Anger

When the chief priests and the scribes saw the wonders that he did and the children shouting in the temple, "Hosanna to the Son of David!" they were indignant.

—Matthew 21:15

The Temple

Read Matthew 21:12-17, 45-46; Matthew 26:1-5.

The Pharisees were religious rulers who cared more about rules and money than they did about showing God's love. When Jesus went to the temple and saw what their hearts were really like, He was angry, which then made the Pharisees angry.

The happiness of Palm Sunday didn't last very long. The day after the Triumphal Entry, Jesus came upon the temple, a place of worship for the Jews and the only place where Gentiles (non-Jews) were allowed to worship. But Jesus instead saw the Jews using the temple as a marketplace, buying and selling things to make money and keeping the Gentiles from worshipping God. Jesus was angry. He flipped tables over, sending money and goods flying! Can you imagine the scene? Then He said, "Is it not written, 'My house will be called a house of prayer for all nations'? But you have made it a den of thieves!" (Mark 11:17). Why did Jesus appear to be so angry?

When Jesus was twelve years old, He went missing from His parents for three days during a journey home from Jerusalem. His parents finally found Him back in the temple with the teachers. His mother, Mary, asked why He had stayed behind, and young Jesus answered, "Didn't you know that it was necessary for me to be in my Father's house?" (Luke 2:49). Even as a boy, Jesus knew the temple was designed as a place of connection with God.

Now, as an adult, Jesus grew angry because the temple was being used as a place to cheat Jews out of money and prevent Gentiles from connecting with God.

Anger and the Temple

While Jesus was in the temple that day, blind and sick people came to Him for healing. Do you know who watched these miracles? Children— just like you! They were amazed by Jesus and shouted the very same praise from the Triumphal Entry the day before: "Hosanna to the Son of David!" (Matthew 21:15). But the Pharisees were "indignant," or very angry, because Jesus was getting attention. And every time they tried to get Jesus to stop people from praising Him, He always answered with Scriptures that the Pharisees knew but weren't following. Jesus was angry because His people were being treated unfairly and being cheated while buying animals for sacrifice; the Pharisees were angry because they thought they were being treated unfairly.

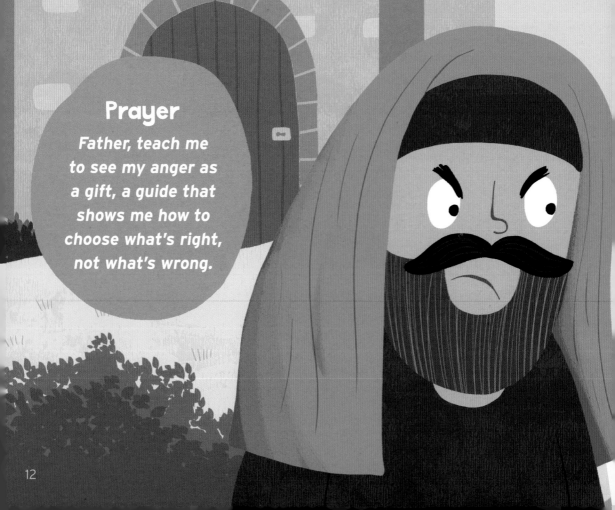

Prayer

Father, teach me to see my anger as a gift, a guide that shows me how to choose what's right, not what's wrong.

Anger

Anger is a secondary emotion, which means there's usually another feeling behind it. Jesus was probably feeling sad that His Father's house was being used selfishly to rob others, build bank accounts, and keep people from worshipping God. The Pharisees, on the other hand, were likely feeling jealous that the people were turning to Jesus for answers instead of them.

During the next two days of Holy Week, Jesus asked the jealous Pharisees questions they couldn't answer and told parables about those who would be rejected by the kingdom of God (Matthew 21:18–23). The Pharisees knew He was talking about them, which only made them angrier. They began planning how they could arrest Jesus.

Family Time Questions

1. Imagine you were there the day Jesus flipped over the tables in the temple and later healed others. Where do you picture yourself in the story?

   _____

   _____

2. What feeling shows up in you as you listen to the story?

   _____

   _____

3. What is the difference between the anger of Jesus that day and the anger of the Pharisees? What does the anger of Jesus lead Him to do? What about the anger of the Pharisees?

   _____

   _____

   _____

4. Read Ephesians 4:26. What do you think this verse means for your life?

   _____

   _____

   _____

5. Is there anything you'd like to say to Jesus right now? Put your words into a prayer to Him.

   _____

   _____

Family Activity

Remote Control

Find an old remote control, or have your children make one with cardboard. The remote is used to teach children how to control their behavior when they get angry. You can use real scenarios in the heat of the moment or imagine scenarios as role play. This game helps your kids problem solve in emotionally driven situations. Here are a few examples:

- Your brother took a toy you were playing with. You push him.
- You want to eat a snack before bedtime, but Mom and Dad say no. You refuse to go to bed.
- While building a tower with blocks, it falls over. You throw the blocks across the room.

Here are what the buttons mean:

Pause: You hit this button before you act. Talk about the behavior you want to take.

Fast-Forward: Hit the fast-forward button to talk about the consequences of a behavior you want to take. What are the consequences of acting this way, both good and bad?

Stop: Hit the stop button if you think the behavior you want to take will cause you to sin in your anger (Ephesians 4:26).

Play: Hit the play button to proceed with the behavior you believe is the right decision. Discuss why you chose this behavior.

Rewind: Use this button to go back and discuss ways you could have behaved differently in a situation where you "flew off the handle." How could a different behavior have resulted in a better outcome?

Volume: Use this button to talk about how loudly you are using your voice. Do you need to turn the volume down?

Mute: Do you need to stop talking? Is what you are saying hurting someone else or making the situation worse?

Channel up / down: Use this button to flip through different behaviors you could take. Discuss the consequences of each of these behaviors.

**Day 3
Feeling:
Gratitude**

"Truly I tell you, wherever this gospel is proclaimed in the whole world, what she has done will also be told in memory of her."

—Matthew 26:13

The Anointing at Bethany

Read Matthew 26:6-13.

In a town called Bethany, a woman named Mary had dinner with Jesus and some of their closest friends. She was so grateful for Jesus and His love for her that she poured a very expensive bottle of perfume on His feet to honor Him.

Jesus was eating with His friends in Bethany. But dinner was interrupted as Mary, the sister of Martha and Lazarus, anointed Jesus with a very expensive perfume. She poured it on Jesus' feet and wiped His feet with her hair (John 12:3).

This whole scene must have been shocking to the other dinner guests! Not only did Mary interrupt dinner, but she also let her hair down and touched Jesus' feet with it. Jewish women rarely took down their hair in public. And the bottle of perfume? It was worth up to a year's salary, so the disciples were upset and scolded Mary for wasting it (Mark 14:5). "This might have been sold for a great deal and given to the poor," Judas said (Matthew 26:8-9).

Unlike the Pharisees, Mary not only knew Jesus was the Messiah, but she was also willing to give everything she had to Him, grateful that He had come to save her. She didn't know it at the time, but she was anointing Jesus' body for His death, which was only days away. Jesus saw her gratitude and honored her faith: "Truly I tell you, wherever this gospel is proclaimed in the whole world, what she has done will also be told in memory of her" (Matthew 26:13).

Gratitude and the Anointing at Bethany

Jesus told His disciples not to scold Mary: "She has done a noble thing for me" (Mark 14:6). Mary was so grateful for Jesus that not even people's opinions or the loss of money could keep her gratitude from overflowing. And Jesus knew the significance of what her actions meant. The perfume would become a symbol of His soon-to-come death and burial (John 12:7).

Prayer

Jesus, today I want to thank You. Thank You for _____ (list 5 things you're grateful for today).

Gratitude

Gratitude is one of the most powerful feelings we can experience. It's a feeling that can push out anxiety and honor others. Paul wrote in Philippians 4:6, "Don't worry about anything, but in everything, through prayer and petition with thanksgiving, present your requests to God." Later in 1 Thessalonians 5:18, he wrote, "Give thanks in everything; for this is God's will for you in Christ Jesus." When we act on our gratitude, we show respect for the good things in our lives, including the people we're thankful for. When Mary acted on her gratitude toward Jesus, she honored Him. And Jesus knew we would remember her for it.

Family Time Questions

1. Imagine you were at the dinner when Mary anointed Jesus with perfume. Where do you picture yourself in the story?

2. What feelings would you have as you watched the scene play out?

3. Share three to five things you're really grateful for right now.

4. Tell a story of a time you acted on your gratitude. Did you tell your parents how grateful you were for them? Or maybe you gave your teacher a small gift to say thank-you. How do you think your act of gratitude made each person feel?

5. Is there anything you'd like to say to Jesus right now? Put your words into a prayer to Him.

_____

_____

_____

_____

_____

Family Activity

I Spy What God Created

This is the classic game of I Spy but with a twist. Have your kids take turns spying something God created. Since God created everything, the game isn't hard. Your kids can really choose just about anything. But what makes this game fun is to discover gratitude for and awe of God's creativity. Whenever somebody spies something, they name it aloud, rather than having someone guess it. Instead of guessing what the person spies, the other people will name why they are grateful God created what the person spies.

For example, "I spy with my little eye a horse." Take turns having others say, "I'm grateful God created a horse because they help farmers plow their fields." Somebody else might say, "I'm grateful God created a horse because they are fun to ride."

The next person could take a turn and say, "I spy with my little eye a house." Though God didn't build the house directly, He created the materials and worked through the people who built it. You can see how anything is game here. Someone might say, "I'm grateful God created houses so we don't get wet when it rains."

Day 4
Feeling:
Surprise

He came to Simon Peter, who asked him, "Lord, are you going to wash my feet?"
—John 13:6

22

The Last Supper

Read Luke 22:14–20; John 13:1–16, 33–35; Matthew 26:26–29.

The Last Supper is when Jesus celebrated Passover and had dinner with the disciples, knowing He would soon die. The night was full of surprises, with Jesus washing the disciples' feet and telling them it would be His last meal.

The Last Supper most likely fell on Thursday of Holy Week. It's called the Last Supper because it was Jesus' last Passover supper on earth before His death the next day (Luke 22:16; Revelation 19:9–10). But none of the disciples knew Jesus was about to die.

Jesus began by telling the disciples, who had spent *all* their time with Him the last three years, that this would be His last meal until the kingdom of God came (Luke 22:16). Imagine what they were thinking: *What does He mean this is His last meal? And when will the kingdom of God come?* He then asked them to drink wine and eat bread to remember Him.

Jesus also told the disciples that someone (Judas Iscariot) would betray Him (read more about that on Day 5). Then came one of the most surprising moments of the Last Supper: Jesus washed everyone's feet. Only servants washed people's feet! Jesus said, "What I'm doing you don't realize now, but afterward you will understand" (John 13:7). Shocked, Peter said, "You will never wash my feet" (v. 8). But Jesus was clear: "If I don't wash you, you have no part with me" (v. 8). The night before He died, Jesus surprised the disciples by showing the incredible humility of their King.

Surprise and the Last Supper

Everything Jesus said and did during the Last Supper felt upside-down to the disciples. *Why was this Jesus' last supper? Is the kingdom of God coming tomorrow? How could one of His friends betray Him? Why is Jesus washing our feet? Shouldn't we be washing His?* They were even more surprised when Jesus gave them a new command: to love others as Jesus loved them—a command for us to love everyone, even if others deny us, betray us, or bully us (John 13:33–35). How's that for surprising? For the last surprising act of the meal, Jesus told Peter that Peter would deny Jesus three times before the rooster crowed. Peter couldn't believe it!

Prayer

Lord Jesus, thank You for surprising us by becoming a servant. Help me to surprise others in my service to them.

Surprise

Surprise is an emotional response to something unexpected. Surprise can be pleasant and welcome (a surprise trip with your family) or it can be unpleasant and not welcome (finding out the trip is canceled). Jesus' disciples began the Passover meal with no idea what would happen that night. Their world was about to get turned upside-down.

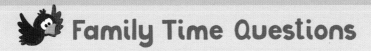# Family Time Questions

1. What part of the story of the Last Supper surprises you the most?

   _____

   _____

   _____

   _____

2. Imagine being at the Last Supper and having Jesus wash your feet. How would you feel?

   _____

   _____

   _____

   _____

3. Tell about a time you were surprised, either pleasantly or unpleasantly.

   _____

   _____

   _____

   _____

4. Which one of Jesus' lessons at the Last Supper is most surprising to you? (A few examples: leaders must be servants, we must love those who don't love us, and the first will be last and the last will be first.)

   _____

   _____

   _____

   _____

5. Is there anything you'd like to say to Jesus right now? Put your words into a prayer to Him.

_____

_____

_____

_____

_____

_____

Family Activity

Serving Well

The foot washing at the Last Supper is a surprising act of humility. Take time to schedule a foot washing in your home. Tie a towel around your waist as Jesus did in John 13. Help your children understand Jesus' desire for us to serve the way He served. Talk about ways you can *surprise* others by how you serve them. Come up with a "bucket list" of two to three ways you can serve your neighbors, family, church family, or community leading up to Easter.

_____

_____

_____

_____

_____

_____

_____

Day 5
Feeling:
Disgust

"The Son of Man will go just as it is written about him, but woe to that man by whom the Son of Man is betrayed! It would have been better for him if he had not been born."

—Mark 14:21

The Betrayal

Read Matthew 26:14–25; Psalm 41:9.

Judas Iscariot was one of the twelve disciples, but he betrayed Jesus and turned Him in to be arrested. Because Judas was one of Jesus' closest friends, his betrayal left everyone feeling upset and disgusted.

As one of the twelve disciples, Judas Iscariot was not only a student but also a friend of Jesus. In the verses right after the anointing at Bethany, Judas sneaked away to meet with the religious leaders, who were feeling angry and jealous toward Jesus. They had ordered that if anyone knew where Jesus was, His location had to be reported so that the leaders could arrest Him (John 11:57). Knowing this, Judas secretly agreed to bring the religious leaders to Jesus in exchange for thirty pieces of silver.

On Thursday afternoon of Holy Week, Jesus sent two disciples into the city to prepare for the Passover. Later that evening, while eating the Passover meal, He said something that upset the disciples: "Truly I tell you, one of you will betray me" (Matthew 26:21). In distress, the disciples began asking, "Surely not I, Lord?" To fulfill Psalm 41:9, Jesus said, "He's the one I give the piece of bread to after I have dipped it" (John 13:26). After dipping the bread, He handed it to Judas. Instead of asking, "Surely not I, *Lord*?" as the other disciples did, Judas asked, "Surely not I, *Rabbi*?" (Matthew 26:25). This means Judas saw Jesus as a teacher, not his Lord.

Disgust and
the Betrayal

When we betray someone, we break their trust. This is what Judas did to Jesus, and Jesus knew it was coming. He said to Judas, "What you're doing, do quickly" (John 13:27). Later that night, Judas brought the religious leaders to the garden of Gethsemane to arrest Jesus. Wanting to pull out swords to defend Jesus, the disciples must have been disgusted to learn that Judas had turned in their friend for money (Luke 22:49–50).

Prayer

Father, I am disgusted by my own sin. Please help me know when my choices hurt my relationship with You.

Disgust

When something disgusts you, you really, really dislike it. Think of the taste of the ickiest food you can imagine. The sound of nails on a chalkboard. Or the smell of dog poop. Disgust touches more than the senses though. When somebody does something to hurt others or is downright evil, we feel disgusted by their behavior. Judas secretly met with the religious leaders, plotted to have Jesus arrested, and then led the soldiers to Him. Judas's behavior wasn't just a mistake. He deliberately planned to have his friend arrested. Ick!

Family Time Questions

1. What part of the story do you dislike the most?

_____

_____

_____

_____

_____

2. What do you think the disciples felt when Jesus said someone at their table would betray Him?

_____

_____

_____

_____

3. Name a few things that are disgusting to you.

_____

_____

_____

_____

4. Have you ever been disgusted by someone else's behavior? Explain.

_____

_____

_____

_____

5. Is there anything you'd like to say to Jesus right now? Put your words into a prayer to Him.

_____

_____

_____

_____

_____

Family Activity

Redeeming Songs

Play and sing a song your kids know. Then ask, "What's this song about? What is it teaching us?" Many kids get caught up in tunes because they elicit a _feeling_. Yet they do so without thinking about or understanding the lyrics. Some song lyrics are about heartbreak and leave you feeling sad or disgusted. Other songs tell stories of heartbreak but leave you feeling redeemed. Use this game to talk about the redemptive value of a song and the message and feeling it leaves us with.

For older kids, you may want to ask what they love listening to and begin there. Perhaps songs from new movies are popular but they haven't listened intently to hear the message of the lyrics. Have them consider: What type of behavior is the song celebrating? What do I feel (sad, happy, disgusted, angry, etc.) after listening to it? What message is the song trying to teach me? For younger kids, you could make it more intentional by singing, "The B.I.B.L.E., yes that's the book for me." Or you could also listen to a favorite preschool song and decide if there's a lesson or if it's just a song for fun.

Day 6
Feeling:
Sadness

Being in anguish, he prayed more fervently, and his sweat became like drops of blood falling to the ground.

—Luke 22:44

The Crucifixion

Read Luke 22:39–53; 22:63–23:49.

A *crucifixion* was when someone died on a cross for committing a crime. Jesus never committed a crime, or a sin, yet was crucified anyway. The heavens and earth were sad the day He died.

Jesus' death on the cross was full of sadness. In the garden of Gethsemane, He prayed that He wouldn't have to go to the cross. But He was ready to do what God the Father wanted so we could be saved from our sins. After praying, He found the disciples "sleeping, exhausted from their grief" (Luke 22:45). Grief is a deep feeling of sadness. Remember all the surprises from the night before? Jesus' disciples were emotionally exhausted.

The sadness continued later that dark night as Judas brought soldiers to Jesus. Jesus was arrested, blindfolded, ridiculed, and beaten. None of the government officials found Jesus guilty, but He was brought before the people, who demanded He be put to death. As He was led away to be crucified, "a large crowd of people followed him, including women who were mourning and lamenting him" (Luke 23:27). A person who is mourning shows sadness. Although many people had demanded that Jesus die, some still believed He was the Messiah and were saddened by all that was happening.

Jesus was nailed to the cross and died. Even the earth was sad. Can you believe that? Not only was there an earthquake, but for three hours in the middle of the day, the world also became completely dark as if the earth was hiding in grief. The crowds walked away, "striking their chests," a public way of showing grief and sadness (Luke 23:48). Some of the people who demanded Jesus be put to death might have had second thoughts and were now sad. And just imagine Jesus' family and close friends watching through their tears as He died. It was a sad day.

Sadness and the Crucifixion

The religious leaders and Roman authorities made fun of Jesus. His loved ones "stood watching" (Luke 23:35, 49). Imagine standing by as someone you love dearly was being humiliated and killed and you could do nothing about it. Imagine the sadness Jesus felt as He hung from the cross, looking at the crowds who had no idea they were putting to death the true Messiah. Even while being treated horribly, Jesus asked the Father to forgive them. The sorrow and grief of this entire day was life changing.

Sadness

Sadness is an emotion that points to loss. It means something important to you is now gone, either temporarily or permanently. Perhaps you've been sad when you had to miss a special event or when your grandparents left after a fun visit. These are temporary losses. But a divorce in the family, the death of a pet, or leaving behind good friends when you move away are permanent losses and lead to grief.

The more you love someone or value something, the more you grieve when it's lost. That's why grief and sadness are actually good. They mean you care deeply. It's no wonder, then, that the people grieved the loss of Jesus. They wondered if they had lost their Master forever.

Prayer

Heavenly Father, You know what it's like to be sad because You lost Your only Son. You understand my loss. Please comfort me in my sadness.

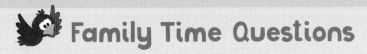

Family Time Questions

1. Jesus asked God to keep Him from dying on the cross. Yet Jesus said He didn't want to do what *He* wanted, but what *God* knew was best instead (Luke 22:42). Why was it important that Jesus obey God?

2. Imagine being in the crowd when the people were yelling to have Jesus killed. How would you feel as you watched someone you loved being treated so unfairly?

3. After Jesus died, people went away "striking their chests," a public way of showing grief and sadness. Have you ever lost something or someone so special that it made you want to scream, kick, or throw something?

4. Remember, to be sad means you have a big heart. It means you care. Read Matthew 5:4. What do you think this verse means?

5. Is there anything you'd like to say to Jesus right now? Put your words into a prayer to Him.

_____

_____

_____

_____

_____

_____

Family Activity

Honoring What We Lost

Have your children draw a picture of a moment they felt sad. What, or who, did they lose? How did they express their sadness? Did they listen to music, go for a walk, talk to a friend or parent? Have your children draw as much detail in the picture as possible to express how they felt about what they lost. Then, after they have colored the picture, have your children draw a picture of Jesus somewhere in the picture. Where do they see Jesus in the middle of their grief?

Once your child has drawn the pictures, find a way together to honor what or who they lost. Perhaps they write a letter or draw a picture to the pet, grandparent, or old school they lost. Or maybe they find a way to honor what they lost with a keepsake in their room. Use this activity to help your children find ways to talk about and express their sadness and honor what they lost.

Day 7
Feeling:

Fear

Mary Magdalene and the other Mary were seated there, facing the tomb.

—Matthew 27:61

The Unknown

Read Matthew 27:57-66.

The day after Jesus died was the Sabbath, or a day of rest, in Israel. Less than a week before, people had happily waved palm branches because Jesus was on earth to save them. Now He was dead, and people were afraid, not knowing what would happen next.

On Friday evening after Jesus died, a rich man named Joseph of Arimathea had offered his own tomb to bury Jesus. After Jesus' body was wrapped in clean linen, Joseph put Him in the tomb and rolled a large stone to close the entrance. "Mary Magdalene and the other Mary were there" (Matthew 27:61).

Imagine these women at the tomb. The tears they cried. The questions they had. The fear they felt. The man so many hoped to be the Messiah was dead. Was He really the Messiah? Why had He not just taken Himself off the cross? What would happen to His disciples, to those who believed in Him? Would the Jewish leaders come after them?

After Jesus' body was left in the tomb, there was an entire Saturday full of the unknown. Not much is written about this particular day in the Bible. It was the Sabbath, but this was a day of rest like none other ever before it, or to ever come after it. Even Jesus' disciples hid for fear of the Jews (John 20:19). Everyone was probably thinking about the unknown of who Jesus was and the fear of what would happen now that He had died.

Fear and the Unknown

When fearful, people either fight the threat or run from it. The religious leaders feared Jesus' message and miraculous works so much that they fought to put Him to death. On the day after Jesus died, they were still so afraid that they went to Pilate, the Roman governor, and asked that the tomb be extra secure so nobody could steal the body. So the Romans sealed the tomb and put a guard in place.

Fear also has a way of making people run and hide. Adam and Eve were afraid and hid from God in the garden of Eden (Genesis 3:8–10). The Israelites were afraid and ran away from Goliath (1 Samuel 17:24). And now, Jesus' disciples ran away when He was arrested (Mark 14:50), and they hid after His death (John 20:19).

Prayer

Father, when I feel scared and alone in unknown moments in my life, help me to run to You and not away from You.

Fear

Fear is a God-given emotion that helps us either fight off a threat or run from the danger. This built-in response of fear is healthy because it keeps us safe. But throughout the Bible, God tells us not to be afraid of people or things but to fear Him instead. When we fear God, we call on, obey, and run to Him. In most other kinds of fear, we run away from Him. How confusing it must have been for the disciples to watch the Son of God die on the cross and to be left alone the next day. No wonder they ran away and hid in fear.

Family Time Questions

1. Imagine yourself in this story. Are you helping Joseph of Arimathea wrap Jesus' body and put Him in the tomb? Are you sitting with the women staring at the tomb? Running away with the disciples in fear? Talk about why you see yourself where you do.

_____

_____

_____

_____

2. What do you think those who believed Jesus was the Messiah were thinking the day after He died?

_____

_____

_____

_____

3. Have you ever run away and hidden when you were scared?

_____

_____

_____

4. Is there anything you'd like to say to God right now? Put your words into a prayer to Him.

_____

_____

_____

_____

5. Write a note today to Jesus about how thankful you are that He died for you.

_____

_____

_____

_____

Family Activity

God's Got It

When we're fearful, it certainly doesn't feel like "God's got it." This activity helps children learn to relax and begin giving their fears to God from an early age.

Begin by asking your kids to name one thing they're afraid of. Ask this question in different ways depending on the age and maturity of your children. "What is one thing you're not looking forward to this week?" "Is there an event coming up you're anxious about?" You could go first as an example.

Hopefully, this activity will help your kids learn to relax when they're feeling fearful or alone:

1. Have your child specifically verbalize his or her fear. (This reduces worry.)
2. Everybody closes their eyes and takes slow deep breaths. (Breathe in to count of four. Hold for count of four. Release to count of eight.)
3. Teach your children to picture their lungs as balloons filled with air. As they slowly "release the fear" from their bodies, picture the Holy Spirit replacing it with peace.
4. Once the person who shared feels more at peace, he begins counting backward aloud from three, two, one, and everybody yells together, "God's got it!" as they open their eyes.

**Day 8
Feeling:**

Joy

So, departing quickly from the tomb with fear and great joy, they ran to tell his disciples the news.

—Matthew 28:8

The Resurrection

Read Matthew 28:1–10; Luke 24:1–12.

The day after the Sabbath, Mary Magdalene and other women went to the tomb early in the morning. But they found the stone rolled away and the tomb empty. Full of great joy, the women ran to tell the others the good news—Jesus had risen from the dead!

Happy Easter! Christ has risen! Can you believe it? It's very difficult for our minds to understand how Jesus could have died and then come back alive again three days later. Even those who saw Jesus in person after He rose from the dead needed time to understand what had happened.

Early Sunday morning, Mary Magdalene and the other women, who remained very faithful to Jesus, went to His tomb while it was still dark. A violent earthquake rocked the area as an angel appeared and rolled the stone away from the entrance of the tomb. The angel told the women, "Don't be afraid. . . . [Jesus] is not here. For he has risen" (Matthew 28:5–6).

After seeing that the tomb was empty, the women ran with great joy to tell the disciples. But the Bible says, "These words seemed like nonsense to them, and they did not believe the women" (Luke 24:11). So Peter ran to the tomb as fast as he could to see it for himself. When Peter and John arrived at the tomb, they, too, saw that it was empty. Peter was amazed! Later, when Jesus showed Himself to the rest of the disciples, "they still were amazed and in disbelief because of their joy" (v. 41). This was just too good to be true! To show that He was indeed alive again, Jesus asked for something to eat, and they gave Him fish. Everything the disciples had hoped for had come true. Jesus was alive, and He still is!

Joy and the Resurrection

Jesus did as He had said—He rose from the dead! This is the most amazing news in the history of the world. "Death has been swallowed up in victory" (1 Corinthians 15:54).

Jesus was made weak for you because He knows every one of your weaknesses. He became sin for you because He knows every one of your sins. He died for you because He knows that without His death, you'd be dead too. And even though He knows your weaknesses, sins, and everything about you, He still loves you! He even delights in you. That is a reason to shout for joy! He died so you could live. And He rose again so He could spend eternity with you. No wonder the Bible tells us over and over again to be joyful!

Prayer

Lord Jesus, You came, bringing joy and peace. Help me live my life so people will ask me the reason for my joy!

Joy

On Day 1 we learned that when life is going well, we feel happy, but when it's not, we don't. Well, joy is different. Life doesn't need to be going well for you to have joy. Joy is what you feel and why you can celebrate when you know "God's got this," no matter what you're going through. You remind yourself that you have victory over your circumstances. You have victory over the enemy. You have victory over death. But living from joy requires faith. Even the disciples needed to see Jesus alive. They needed to see how real He was. They needed to experience Him. And so do you.

 Family Time Questions

1. Have you ever seen something so joyful and amazing that you had a hard time believing it was true?

_____

_____

_____

_____

2. Imagine you were there at the resurrection. Where do you most see yourself in the story? At the tomb in the dark with the women? Arriving with Peter and John? What are you feeling when you first discover the tomb is empty?

_____

_____

_____

_____

3. Describe a time you were filled with joy. Have you *felt* the joy of Jesus and experienced His presence?

_____

_____

_____

_____

4. How has the joy you have for God's goodness spilled over to help others?

_____

_____

_____

_____

5. Is there anything you'd like to say to Jesus right now? Put your words into a prayer to Him.

_____

_____

_____

_____

_____

Family Activity

A Family of Joy

Take turns talking about what activities fill each family member with joy. For example, somebody might feel joyful having dinner at a restaurant that means something special to your family. Somebody else might feel joyful simply going for a walk. Or perhaps others feel joyful playing board games, sitting by a campfire, or having a family dance party.

As you come up with your list, go do one thing together that brings your family joy. Don't be afraid to celebrate *big* and make a beautiful memory of remembering Jesus' resurrection together!

Day 9
Feeling:
Remorse

He went outside
and wept bitterly.
—Matthew 26:75

Peter's Restoration

Read Matthew 26:69–75; Luke 5:1–11; John 21:1–19.

Peter loved Jesus dearly and fought for Him. But before Jesus died, Peter denied knowing Him three times. Since Jesus knew Peter was remorseful, meaning he was truly sorry for what he had done, Jesus restored His relationship with Peter after rising from the dead.

Peter first met Jesus years earlier after a long night of fishing but catching nothing. As Peter cleaned his nets that morning, Jesus told him to throw his nets out one more time. Peter and his partners caught so many fish the boats began to sink! He fell at Jesus' knees and said, "Go away from me, because I'm a sinful man, Lord" (Luke 5:8). Peter called Jesus "Lord" at this first meeting. From that point on, Peter was ready to fight for Him.

Peter was often extra enthusiastic and emotional when it came to serving his Lord. At the Last Supper, Jesus predicted that Peter would deny Him three times. Peter reacted, "Lord . . . I'm ready to go with you both to prison and to death" (Luke 22:33). But only a few hours later, Peter would refuse three times to admit that he knew Jesus. Then, as Jesus had predicted, the rooster crowed, and Peter cried.

Can you imagine what Peter felt after Jesus died? It's no surprise he sprinted to the tomb to see if it was indeed empty.

Though Jesus had appeared to the disciples twice already, Peter hadn't had the chance to talk to Him and instead goes back to fishing. And what happens? Jesus sought out Peter and once again showed up after a night when Peter had caught no fish. He invited Peter to have breakfast on the shore. During breakfast, Jesus restored Peter's relationship with Him. Once again, as He did the day they had met, He said to Peter, "Follow me" (John 21:19).

Remorse and Peter's Restoration

The Bible says, "All have sinned and fall short of the glory of God" (Romans 3:23). Peter was no different. He, too, was a sinner. But there was a big difference between Peter and Judas. Remember when Judas betrayed Jesus? Though Judas felt remorse (Matthew 27:3), he never once called Jesus "Lord," or confessed his sin to Jesus as the Messiah. But Peter did. Peter knew Jesus was the Messiah. When Jesus sought him out, Peter's remorse led him to repent and turn from his cowardly ways. Although Peter would mess up many more times in his life (see Galatians 2:11–14 as one example), he always knew he could repent and be restored, and that Jesus was eagerly ready to forgive him.

Prayer

Lord Jesus, keep my heart soft and remorseful when I sin. Create in me a pure heart, and forgive me.

Remorse

Remorse is when you feel bad for something you did wrong. Just like Peter, "If you confess with your mouth, 'Jesus is Lord,' and believe in your heart that God raised him from the dead, you will be saved" (Romans 10:9). When you believe with your heart, the Holy Spirit guides you to do what is right (v. 10). So when you've done something wrong, and you feel sick about what you've done, that's a really good feeling to have. It means you're paying attention to how Jesus wants you to live. All you need to do is confess your sin to God and turn away from doing it again. Since He is your Lord, He will restore you back to Himself every time.

Family Time Questions

1. After reading the three Bible stories for Day 9, what did you notice about the way Jesus interacted with Peter? Describe everything that stands out to you.

_____

_____

_____

_____

2. Read Matthew 26:69–75 again. Imagine yourself in the story. Are you in the crowd watching Peter deny that he knows Jesus? Are you Peter, afraid to tell others that you believe in and know Jesus? Or are you someone who is questioning other people about their relationship with Jesus?

_____

_____

_____

_____

3. Can you relate to Peter after the rooster crows? Describe how Peter is likely feeling as he "weeps bitterly."

_____

_____

_____

_____

4. Have you ever experienced remorse? Talk about a time you felt really bad for something you did wrong. How did you make it right? Did someone have to forgive you?

_____

_____

_____

_____

_____

5. Have you felt remorseful for your sins toward God? Would you like to ask Him now for forgiveness?

_____

_____

_____

_____

_____

Family Activity

Family Poem

Spend time writing a poem about Jesus' death and resurrection. Poems often describe feelings. You can describe how Jesus' death and resurrection makes you feel. You can write individual poems or make it a family poem you can have as a keepsake. Spend time throughout the month putting together your poem. Try to use feeling words in your poem to describe when you felt sad, remorseful, happy, or joyful because of Jesus' death and resurrection. When you're done, recite the poem together. Another fun option is to frame it and hang it on your wall.

Day 10
Feeling:
Bravery

"Go, therefore, and make disciples of all nations, baptizing them in the name of the Father and of the Son and of the Holy Spirit, teaching them to observe everything I have commanded you."
—Matthew 28:19–20

58

The Disciples' Call

Read Matthew 28:16-20.

Jesus rose from the dead, but He didn't stay on earth with His disciples forever. He sent the Holy Spirit to be on earth while He went back to heaven. Before He left, He told the disciples to bravely tell the world all about Him.

After the resurrection, Jesus appeared to the disciples several times and "to over five hundred brothers and sisters at one time" (1 Corinthians 15:6). He ate with the disciples, showed them the scars on His hands, and forgave Peter. But some of the disciples still doubted and had a hard time believing Jesus was alive. Knowing their doubt, Jesus told them that "all authority," not just some authority, but "*all* authority has been given to [Him] in heaven *and* on earth" (Matthew 28:18). He commanded them to tell the world all about Him, and then He ascended—meaning He was taken up—into heaven and was seated at the right hand of God. He is there to this day (Mark 16:19).

For the disciples, this was a powerful moment, and it's one that matters for you as well. Jesus holds all authority, meaning He has the power to overcome evil, forgive people of their sins, and lead them into a new life fully alive forever and ever. Through our faith in Him, we, too, have been given His authority to go out into the world to disciple, baptize, and teach others to follow His commands. Sounds amazing, right?

After Jesus' ascension, the disciples went out and began preaching the good news of Jesus' resurrection (Mark 16:20). After everything that had happened—the chief priests and Pharisees arresting Jesus, the crowds demanding He die, and the empty tomb—the disciples were now bravely out in public doing what Jesus commanded. These were the same disciples who, just weeks before, had scattered and hid and denied even knowing Him. Now they were taking the authority they had through their faith in Jesus to tell everyone about Him!

Bravery and the Disciples' Call

Telling others about Jesus is not always easy. Not everybody knows Jesus or wants to follow His commands. As humans, we want to do whatever we want. It's a rebellion that began with Adam and Eve. So when people hear what they have to give up to follow Jesus, many don't like it. But God knows what's best for us. He loves us so much that He wants to protect us. Jesus knows that without Him, we will die; but with Him, we live fully alive forever and ever. He calls you to bravely share this message just like the disciples did: "God loved the world in this way: He gave his one and only Son, so that everyone who believes in him will not perish but have eternal life" (John 3:16).

Prayer

Father, help me to be strong and courageous as I tell others about Your love.

Bravery

Being brave doesn't mean you don't feel afraid; it means you choose to act even if you feel scared. After Jesus told the disciples to go into the world to make disciples, baptize, and teach, He said, "Remember, I am with you always" (Matthew 28:20). Years and years before, God had commanded Joshua, "Be strong and courageous. Do not be afraid or discouraged, for the LORD your God is with you wherever you go" (Joshua 1:9). Just like Joshua and the disciples, you can be brave and share God's love with others because He is with you.

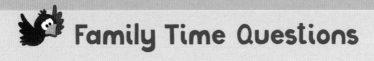 Family Time Questions

1. Do you think you'd be one of the disciples who still doubted that Jesus was alive again? Are there times today you doubt Him?

_____

_____

_____

_____

_____

2. Have you ever been afraid to share your faith with others? If so, what made it so difficult?

_____

_____

_____

_____

_____

3. Imagine being one of the disciples after Jesus went back to heaven. What would you feel as you started preaching in public, especially after hiding just days before?

_____

_____

_____

_____

_____

4. When have you been brave?

_____

_____

_____

_____

_____

5. Is there anything you'd like to say to Jesus right now? Put your words into a prayer to Him.

_____

_____

_____

_____

Family Activity

The Brave Family

On a drive or around the dinner table, share how family members see bravery in each other. Follow up with a story of a time you saw their courage in action. Take turns sharing your insights with one another. You can also add to the activity by having each person answer the question about themselves: "What makes me brave?" Or they could answer the question: "What is the greatest strength I bring to our family team?" They could also complete the sentence: "The one thing I love best about our family is . . ." Then share one way you can bravely share the love of Jesus with someone else this week.

For we do not have a high priest who is unable to sympathize with our weaknesses, but one who has been tempted in every way as we are, yet without sin.

—Hebrews 4:15